# Understanding the Heart Origins and Some Relevant Explanations for Male Pornography Addiction

Thomas D. Sharts M.Ed

# Understanding the Heart Origins and Some Relevant Explanations for Male Pornography Addiction

Thomas D. Sharts M.Ed

| Library of Congress Control Number: | | 2016917690 |
|---|---|---|
| ISBN: | Hardcover | 978-1-5245-5387-6 |
| | Softcover | 978-1-5245-5386-9 |
| | eBook | 978-1-5245-5385-2 |

Print information available on the last page.

Rev. date: 11/09/2016

**To order additional copies of this book, contact:**
Xlibris
1-888-795-4274
www.Xlibris.com
Orders@Xlibris.com
751975

# Contents

# Introduction

The need for writing this book is substantial in reference to social relevance. Today in the United States alone, the pornography industry has been estimated to be anywhere from ten to fifteen billion dollars a years in consumptive spending. Globally, the porn industry is estimated to be taking in almost 100 billion dollars a year in consumptive spending. The pornography industry is chiefly comprised of those participating in/or utilizing prostitution, escort services, strip clubs, pornographic magazines, videos, and Internet sites etc. for the purpose of achieving a number of spiritual, physiological, psychological, social and vocational needs. However, the focus of this book will be upon understanding the male pornographic heart and mind (ages:18-up) and what motivates addiction to pornography use – specifically: the perusing of Internet porn sites, pornographic videos or pornographic magazines for realizing spiritual, physiological, psychological, social and vocational needs. In addition, the analysis and commentary in this book regarding male pornography use and abuse is focused upon those male populations residing in the United States.

Ultimately, the writing of this book is for the purpose of achieving the goal of realizing healing for the male pornography user and/ or addict. However, healing can only be realized when a man has become educated in reference to all of those variables that are related to explaining why he needs to continue to use/abuse pornography to meet certain spiritual, physiological, psychological, social and vocational needs. Likewise, once a comprehensive understanding of those variables has been realized, only then can a male porn abuser begin to embrace and implement constructive methods for realizing healing. Likewise, only then, will he be free to live and love in this world and not be a slave to the sexual lusts associated with this world.

If you're a male pornography addict, act now in order to begin your journey toward a whole, healthy and free life! It's never too late! If you're a young male maybe only eighteen, twenty or twenty-five-years of age, don't think this book and its educative message doesn't apply to you! It certainly does, and if you don't extricate yourself from your pornographic addictive ways now, thirty years will pass by and you will still be a slave to your insatiable love for pornography – forsaking and shipwrecking your love relationships, family, employment and vocational opportunities along the way in galore style! Equally, if your porn addiction continues unabated, one day you'll wake-up and look at yourself in the mirror and realize the naked truth: you're a forty-five or fifty-year-old something pervert; and that's the truth about what you truly are and where you have been!

So, what will today bring: more imprisonment and folly to pornography or a new lease on life? Your current and future health depends on you to make an informed decision to do what's right and best for you! Therefore, go ahead and have the courage to read about yourself!

# Chapter 1
## Pornography Addiction

## Defining Pornography

Any erotic thought, viewed image or the fantasizing of a person (male or female) and/or adoration of a sexual object of affection (female breasts, lips, buttocks, vagina, anus, legs or male/female penis, etc.) attached to a person of affection or unattached to a person - for the purpose of achieving a sense of intimacy or sexual orgasm. Some pornographic thoughts, images or fantasies also may humiliate or debase both male and female human beings (Sharts, 2015).

## Is Pornography Addiction a Social Problem?

Pornography is both a macro (regional, national and global) and micro (individual) social problem. There are male pornography abusers in every nation of the world and each male person's individual case of addiction is a social problem for himself – complicating and destroying his life in all of the *areas of being human* formerly cited and harming other people relationally associated with himself.

## Defining Addiction

A male individual is considered a pornography addict when he utilizes pornography as the primary means favored or utilized (in lieu of living persons) to achieve an orgasmic experience. Also, a pornography addiction is further defined and diagnosed when the male abuser of pornography forsakes work, family or educational responsibilities to achieve orgasm through the utilization of pornography. In this book, it will be assumed that designated abusers are also addicts and both descriptions are being utilized with the intention of comprehending the understanding that if a male person is *abusing pornography* it's more than likely he is an *addict to pornography.* Moreover, when I cite *pornography abuse,* the definition is to include the frequency of viewing behavior - which is the observing of pornography on a daily basis – at least once per day for an hour or more.

In truth, pornography addiction is fueled by deprivations in any of the five areas of being human. Those five areas of being human are: spiritual, physiological, sociological, psychological and vocational. From a spiritual perspective, the Almighty Lord God confirms man's inability to live as a perfected being by asking humankind one imperative question: "who has kept his heart pure?"(Proverbs 21:9). In reference to man's physiological and psychological desires, the Old Testament Bible refers to addictive behaviors as: "the roving appetite." (Ecclesiastes 6:9). It also says: "the eye has never seen enough." (Ecclesiastes 1:8).

In addition, any addictive behavior must be understood as a behavior repeated over and over again without cessation that is fueled by deprivations in any of the five areas of being human. Likewise, the porn-addicted male person derives meaning and temporary relief in correlation with a specific area of deprivation (ex: mistrust, hate, anger, guilt, need for power, need for self-affirmation, etc.). This meaning and temporary relief is realized by utilizing a depicted image or expansive video image(s) (homosexuality, intercourse, rape, sodomy, personal stripping and masturbation, sex with animals, male or female fellatio, female or male ejaculation facials, pedophilia, defecation or urination, etc.) in order to accentuate meaning and relief toward that area of deprivation by achieving orgasmic pleasure and a sense of personal security in association with the meaning given to the image or images viewed – a sort of temporary state of healing that must be repeated over and over again – hence reinforcing the addiction and the experiencing of any self-destructive consequences associated with the addiction.

## Is Pornography Addiction a Mental Illness?

Because pornography addiction is an obsession and compulsion, it certainly therefore should be defined as a mental illness.

# How Should Male Pornography Addiction be Understood?

Male pornography addiction must be analyzed and understood from all of the five areas of being human. For instance, all five areas of being human need to be assessed and analyzed in order to understand what deprivations are being experienced in association with motivating the addiction to pornography.

# The Five Areas of Being Human and Explanations for Understanding the Origins of Male Pornography Addiction

## Spiritual Origins: The Heart

In truth, because an individual cannot experience the fullness of the love of God consistently in his/her life, he/she is unable to maintain a perpetual state of wholeness (holiness) in order to overcome the debilitating deprivations he/she experiences in any of the five areas of being human (Roman 7:15-20). That said, we then begin to understand that male pornography addiction is a coping mechanism because of the fact the fullness of the love of God cannot be apprehended consistently enough by the male porn addict in order to overcome the areas of deprivations being experienced. Moreover, from a spiritual point of view, it is a factual belief that Almighty God is in heaven and humankind is upon earth. Although the Holy Spirit is upon earth to help us, human beings are still confined to a physical body that limits our spiritual, physiological, sociological, psychological and vocational understanding; thereby keeping us in an everlasting state of ignorance and bondage to any deprived needs we possess in any of the former-cited areas of being human. Likewise, our spiritual ignorant state energizes us to see many events in the extreme and also motivates many people to act excessively in reference to real or perceived deprivations. The Old Testament gives credibility to this spiritual debilitating fact of the human condition by admonishing us to avoid all extremes. (Ecclesiastes 9:3). Another reason why some males become pornography addicts is because they simply want to test the extremes and limits of the lust associated with forbidden taboo behaviors. Lastly, the male pornography abuser becomes a prisoner to what he is bound by - thereby perpetuating a vicious cycle of madness as cited by Solomon (Ecclesiastes 9:3).

# Physiological Origins

The powerful male animal instinct of sexual desire and urgency is natural because of the need for procreation in reference to surviving the human race forward into perpetuity. However, if a male does not fulfill such urgent sexual desires for procreation, often times other avenues (such as pornography abuse) will be utilized to fulfill the need to create a passionate experience of simulated procreation. Unfortunately, when not experiencing the perennial fullness of the Love of God, the male physical body and its sexual urges cannot be placed under any man's full-submission.

Also, human energy for good (such as procreation) is supposed to be naturally-released; yet, if such release does not occur – an individual experiences inversion of sexual energy – whereby physical debilitating symptoms might occur such as: high blood pressure, acne, acne inversa, skin bleeding, various gastrointestinal disorders, the manifestation of other addictive behaviors, etc.

# Sociological Origins

## Historical

Some males resort to the abuse of pornography in order to: 1) compensate for a lack of historical intimate experiences with their mother; 2) to recreate a historical occurrence of love and intimacy that was experienced with their mother when they were young; 3) to recreate the unmet fantasy-based passion they had for a specific anatomical object of sexual affection or for a certain female or male object of sexual affection when they were in elementary, junior high or high school; 4) to relive the passion of an actual sexual experience realized in the past; and/or 5) to compensate for a lack of historical intimate-affectionate sexual relationships with any person.

## Social Structural

Some males abuse pornography because they either have never had sexual relations with a female or male or their current sexual experiences are unfulfilling - whether as a single or married person. Also, some males may abuse pornography in order to overcome past sexual rejection from a desired person of sexual affection that holds a high-standing in their mind. Or, some males abuse pornography to fulfill circumvented natural sexual urgings of childhood for a personal object of sexual affection that is taboo: a brother, mother, father, sister, aunt, uncle, etc. Alternatively, other males may resort to the abuse of pornography because they fear sexual intimacy and do not desire sexual intimacy at all. Likewise, pornography may serve to fulfill the passion of sexual urgency with no social-strings attached! Some married men abuse pornography because their wife is perceived by them as unattractive and/or the wife views her body in a shameful way, thereby inhibiting her ability to perform in an alluring sexual way. Or, some men abuse pornography as an option for sexual relief because they are surrounded by beautiful women all day-long at work. Lastly, some males may abuse pornography because they don't have an eligible girl or guy present in their interactive lives that they passionately adore or that demonstrates the same level of passionate affection toward them in return. In other words, these males are experiencing limited sexual and intellectual chemistry with an adored partner.

## Cultural

Some males abuse pornography because natural urgings during childhood for sexual intimacy with a person of sexual affection were circumvented as a result of cultural norms or laws forbidding certain taboo sexual actions or sexual relationships from existing; therefore, pornography abuse is currently utilized by them to help overcome the hostility associated with the denial of this natural sexual energy toward that designated person of sexual affection. For example, some males report a sexual love for a sister or relative (that could never be realized because of taboo cultural laws) as a source of anger, guilt and shame – powerful emotions that can only be relieved through the abuse of pornography. Also, in the United States, there are far more women in work-related power roles or increasing in their access to hold power over men - thereby creating a great sense of humiliation for many males that inevitably requires some kind of *under the radar* psychological response to reassure their manhood. In such a case scenario, pornography abuse provides the perfect vehicle for such a psychological elixir in response to females increasing power over men. Moreover, many other nations have cultural ways of life that do not censor images or messages that exalt the female or male body as a sexual object of affection; in fact, many mainstream national cultures overkill in presentation such images and messages thereby energizing males to be consumed with images and thoughts connected to sexual lust and behaviors (Sharts, 2007). Consequently, some males react in a hostile way to the overkill of imagery and messages that suggest that women's bodies are entities to be worshipped! Lastly, another cultural explanation for male pornography abuse is that present-day civilized societies evolved from hunting and gathering societies - groups where humans were almost living like animals - specifically 1) wearing minimal or no clothing; 2) adult males sleeping with underage girls; 3) adult females sleeping with underage males; 4) groups of people likely participating in orgies; and 5) males and females watching each other bathe, urinate, defecate, etc. Likewise, the animal origins of being human are still a part of every male's genetic and physiological make-up that has never disappeared since humanity has evolved into a so-called *civilized society* – hence male pornography abuse may also be an effort to reconcile with the animal desires *deep within* and placate those free and passionate longings for pure lust without civil restraint!

## Economic

The pornography industry is big business and some males are involved with such commerce activity because it is very profitable to do so! Therefore, in some instances, a pornography addiction is fueled by the profitability associated with being involved with pornography as an enterprising business.

## Political

Political reality has to do with stake (goal) issues associated with relationships or as identified within someone's mind. Equally, males may hold multitudinous goals associated with pornography abuse such as: the humiliation of a particular person of sexual affection; a sense of fantasy-based power over a sexual object or person of sexual affection; lusting for purity; overcoming boredom; searching for meaning and intimacy; achieving sexual orgasm with a fantasized person of sexual affection, etc.

## Environmental

Some males are living in isolated geophysical environments where there are minimal social interactive experiences with other persons - thereby easily explaining why the use of pornography might morph into an addictive experience. Or, some males have been born, raised or currently live in a social environment where parents were or currently are open or closeted pornography users/abusers. Also, the growth of cities, mega-malls and more women in the workplace has placed a greater number of females in relational opportunities in geo-proximity to men - thereby increasing a male's need to stave-off real-life potential sexual encounters and/or temptations through the utilization of pornography to relieve sexual frustration and/or stress through fantasy.

# Other Sociological Explanations of Deprivation or Deviance Related to Male Pornography Use and Abuse

### Social Isolation/Social Rejection

A male person might be living in a geo-physical environment where he is isolated or in a social environment where he is socially rejected for a number of reasons – specifically due to: the absence of prestige;

a lack of significant statuses-held; holding a criminal record, etc.; being labeled as a social loser; facing bigotry or prejudices, etc. Consequently, pornography use or abuse provides an opportunity to relieve sexual urges or serves to channel anger issues related to social rejection.

## Boredom

Some males have too much time on their hands – either as a result of being a teenager, having limited work responsibilities or being retired, etc. Correspondingly, having too much time on one's hands allows the mind to wander and in certain instances, lustful thoughts transform into more concrete behavioral choices for realizing sexual pleasure – specifically the use or abuse of pornography.

## Anomie

Some males are living in life circumstances where they are not involved in any meaningful intimate friendships, sexual relationships or vocational experiences. Therefore, pornography use or abuse may serve as a pleasurable outlet for allaying the anger and pain associated with experiences of anomie.

## Substance Abuse

Some males are involved with the usage of certain substances that heighten the perceptual senses associated with experiencing sexual orgasmic pleasure. Similarly, pornography is utilized or abused by males in conjunction with specific substances in order to experience and/or heighten sexual orgasm.

## Social Injustice

The male person might hold anger issues from past failed interactions with objects of sexual affection (real or imagined anatomical or personal). Fantasy-based behaviors practiced through pornography use or abuse serves to allay the angered emotional state through humiliation of the object of affection.

### Limited Status Opportunities

Similar to the motivating force associated with boredom, a male person might use or abuse pornography because he has limited status opportunities afforded to him to validate his personhood along with the fact that actually *not having anything constructive to do on a daily basis* contributes to mass boredom and meaninglessness. Likewise, use and/or abuse of pornography serves as a relieving distraction.

### Immaturity

A male individual might resort to pornography use or abuse as a coping mechanism simply because he lacks life experience to comprehend what other viable options exist in order to manage social or psychological episodes of communal and sexual frustration or to procure a sense of pleasure.

## Social/Psychological Origins: Some Emotional Explanations for Male Use or Abuse of Pornography

### Jealousy/Powerlessness

Some males use or abuse pornography because they are jealous that a certain person of sexual affection or a specific gender of sexual affection holds sexual powers that he cannot ever match, experience or conquer.

### Anger/Hate

Some behavioral acts of using and abusing pornography are correlated with accentuating or relieving anger toward a specific person of sexual affection – whether historical or within present-tense reality.

### Fear

Some males are fearful of being involved in a genuine sexual relationship due to performance anxiety (either substantiated through past failures to achieve an erection or provide a partner with pleasure) as a result of irrational fears or assumptions about future sexual performance.

## Esteem

Some males use or abuse pornography because their low self-esteem prevents them from ever entering into/or sustaining a healthy sexual relationship; therefore, the use and abuse of pornography serves as a fantasy-based outlet for gaining access to any sexual experiences such males desire with any type of person they desire.

# Vocational Origins

A vocation is defined as an individual's calling or purpose in life. This purpose might relate to work, hobbies, family, community, leisure or relationships. Many addictive behaviors – including male pornography addiction – relate to the following facts: 1) people perceive their own lives as meaninglessness, and 2) much of that perception of worthlessness is associated with an ignorance regarding a personal vocation or a loss of purpose or status-held. A good example of a loss of status-held might be those middle-age men who are experiencing unemployment or underemployment and a loss of family economic leadership as a result. In addition, some males who use or are addicted to pornography have little understanding of their own personal vocation. Therefore, with little or zero life purpose to preoccupy their time and energy, some males fall victim to pornography use and/or abuse in order to fill such a void.

In summation, there are far more theoretical explanations for understanding the origins of what motivates males to become users and abusers of pornography than those already identified. However, what has been importantly recognized are those key analytical tools of analysis that are significant for understanding the origins of why male pornography use or abuse might occur. Those critical tools of analysis are the five areas of being human: spiritual, physiological, sociological, psychological and vocational.

# Chapter 2
## Analysis of Some Male Pornographic Preferences

The following delineation is a brief analysis of some preferences that males have for different types of pornography abuse along with providing some theoretical explanations for such choices. Be aware of the fact that all five areas of being human should be considered when determining explanations for the origins of pornographic behaviors preferred by males that use or abuse pornography. Below I have offered some explanations for the origins of such behavioral preferences. However, this analysis is certainly not exhaustive. A trained therapeutic counselor should conduct a thorough analysis utilizing the five areas of being human (cited earlier) in order to fully assess and understand the origins of such pornographic behavioral preferences.

## Voyeurism

All male pornography abuse can be understood as encompassing voyeurism because nudity is gazed upon by the abuser whether in secret or in a public setting - specifically if he is attending a strip club, nudist camp or nudity contest. The motivational origin of male voyeurism maybe correlated with the abuser's need to perceive a sexual object of affection or an attractive person of sexual desire (female or male) in a humiliated and/or exposed state. Or, the male abuser's need to realize the voyeuristic experience maybe related to helping him relieve sexual frustration toward attractive persons of sexual desire that he cannot possess in reality. Voyeurism may also serve to assist males with having access to power over sexual objects or persons of sexual affection or to relieve the psychological contradiction (simultaneous love and hate) that they feels toward sexual objects of affection or persons of sexual affection. For instance, it's likely that much of what motivates the voyeurism associated with male abuse of pornography is his simultaneous love and hate for sexual objects or persons of sexual affection. On the one hand, the male porn abuser admires and loves a sexual object or person of sexual affection for being so sexually attractive and alluring to him; yet on the other hand, he hates the object of sexual affection or person of sexual affection for the fact that the sexual object or male/female person of sexual affection is motivating his sexual lust. Meanwhile, the male porn addict knows that in reality, he will never possess the sexual object or sexual person of affection because he is either not socially competent to possess the sexual object or person of affection (the person of sexual affection is out his league), or sexually possessing the person of sexual affection is taboo! Some examples of female objects of personal affection that males might desire to observe in a nude and/or humiliated state might be: a coworker; a sister; a cousin; an aunt; a girlfriend's friend; a neighbor's wife; a bank teller; a grocery clerk, a teacher; a boss or work-related superior; a movie star; an anchor women; a VIP; a fellow student; the little girl next door; a niece, etc.

## Lust: The Idolatry of Beauty

According to the book of Proverbs in the Old Testament Bible, "the eyes are never satisfied." (Proverbs 27:20). In light of that truthful wisdom, it's easy to understand then why males (depending upon the sexual choice of beauty) cannot get enough of looking at beautiful women or men. Moreover, in the global community we live within today, the 21st century offers males access to any type of human beauty imaginable as a result of not only global travel but also as a consequence of highly advanced mass communications networks that transmit images via mediums such as: print media, television, cinema and the Internet (Sharts 2007). Therefore, if a male desires to fixate upon the beauty of any human being, then, the world and its technology offers him the ability to do so as often as he likes - even to the point of obsession and addiction! Moreover, in reference to female imagery of beauty, many global communities of culture and media have idolized the depiction of female body parts or her sexual allure to the point of mass overkill; furthering along and justifying a male's need and desire to find relief and resolve from such an onslaught of sexual overkilled imagery (Sharts 2007). The result of this overkill of imagery (idolatry) associated with the female body is what the Book of Psalms in the Old Testament Bible describes as "vile." For today, in reference to female overkill of beauty: "what is vile is honored." (Psalm 12:8).

## Nudity and Humiliation

Some male porn addicts prefer to see women or men depicted in solitary nude poses or scenes without any additional characters. This desired preference is focused upon any environmental situation or scene that fully humiliates the posed individual woman or man apart from what natural position of power his/her beauty might command in the real world of social life and circumstances. Those female poses or scenes most desired by males to be observed in order to achieve orgasm are: full frontal nudity; personal masturbation and ejaculation scenes; stripping scenes; personal urination and defecation scenes; a woman or man fully nude in common everyday settings; shower or bathing scenes; females spreading their labia or anus; females sucking their own nipples; females fingering their own vagina or anus; females shaving their pubic hair, etc. Some male porn addicts have reported that they have even placed pictures of nude female bodies over the photographed clothed bodies of various female persons of sexual affection in order to either humiliate the object of sexual affection or fantasize how the fully-clothed female might appear in the nude. In summation, the primary motivating factor for viewing these type of pornographic images described here is to humiliate a sexual person of affection. The humiliation preference might be inspired by past sexual abuse, historical rejection experiences or to realize revenge in relation to any past hurts or social rejection inflicted upon the male abuser of porn.

## Body Part Obsessions, Body Types, Age, Races and Humiliation

Some male pornography abusers are addicted to viewing certain female or male body parts. In reference to viewing naked females, some males favor big-breasted women, others prefer observing any of the following woman's body parts: naked vagina; hairy or shaved vagina; clitoris, anus, etc. This obsession with female body parts maybe related to past experiences where meaning and intimacy was derived through intimate exposure to a particular female body part. Some other preferential experiences may have derived through lovemaking or through specific past cases of sexual abuse. In addition, some male porn addicts secretly wish they were female and possessed the sexual organs of a female, and this obsession and curiosity carries on with the addicted viewing of such preferred female body parts. In reference to male porn addicts viewing other manly body parts, some males are addicted to viewing other males' penises or anus. This type of addicted behavior as well, might be related to past lovemaking experiences or historical sexual abuse.

Also, some male pornography abusers prefer viewing certain body types of females or males; specifically: athletic, slim, voluptuous, plump, adolescent, mature or old. The preference of *body type* is more than likely related to meaning derived as *intimate* through past sexual experiences or abuse.

In reference to age, some male pornography addicts enjoy viewing females or males of various ages such as: children, preteens, teens, or females or males in their twenties, thirties, forties, fifties or above. This age preference is probably related to any pleasurable experiences of observing a naked female or male of a certain age as a result of such observations being made during a very impressionable age and/or time of passionate longing or fantasy. There might also have been an image fixation in relation to a fantasy-based age desire for intimacy or such an experience of intimacy had already occurred. Or this preference for a certain age maybe related to a fantasy that a male porn addict possesses to view a desired aged naked female or male due to curiosity or jealousy associated with the alluring power of a real sexual object of affection in his life.

In reference to preference for race, some male pornography users and abusers predilection for viewing naked females or males of a certain race is related primarily to fantasy. In others words, the male might desire sexual intimacy with a specific race as a result of curiosity or to affirm past sexual fantasy desires for lovemaking with a distinct race of person. Or, the male porn addict might be powerfully enamored by the sexual magnetism that a particular race of person holds in motivating his sexual desire for lovemaking. Or some male porn addicts are trying to reaffirm and relive past sexual experiences of meaning with a particular race of person.

Lastly, some male users and abusers of pornography simply desire to view naked females or males of specific body types, ages or race in order to accentuate humiliation toward the sexual object or person of sexual affection. In one aspect, the male is obsessed with the sexual actor's beauty; yet in another facet, he is utilizing his viewing of pornography as a way of releasing his anger toward his desired sexual object or person of sexual affection by observing the object or person of sexual affection in a humiliated and vulnerable state; a state of vulnerability where he the observer is able to access - what in reality he cannot ever possess - and to punish the sexual object(s) or person of sexual affection that holds sexual power over him; a power that might be leaving him psychologically and physiologically tormented and impotent.

## Sexual Intercourse, Cunnilingus or Fellatio

Some male abusers of pornography enjoy viewing females or males having standard sexual intercourse, anal intercourse or receiving or administering cunnilingus or fellatio. One of the major explanations for such viewing behavior is to vicariously experience intimacy and power simultaneously. Or some male (especially virgins) are curious to understand those sexual techniques that excite males or females in reference to any of those sexual acts delineated above. In addition, some males are especially drawn to voyeurism and enjoy placing themselves in the male actor's experience of either giving or receiving sexual pleasure. Lastly, some male porn addicts enjoy viewing any of the above sexual acts because it may remind them of some historical pleasurable sexual events they experienced with a female, male or multiple sexual partners in the past.

## Taboo/Fetishes

Some male abusers of pornography are motivated to view various taboo and/or fetish behaviors. All of the following taboo/fetish behaviors cited are not of the societal mainstream norm and are considered deviant and taboo in most global mainstream cultures:

Observing males or females eating feces; observing males or females drinking urine; viewing females or males urinating on self or other persons; observing males or females in the act of defecation or defecating on other persons; viewing males or females with semen on their faces or body; observing males or females having sexual relations with animals; viewing a mother and daughter having sexual relations; observing males having sexual relations with other males; observing females having sexual relations with other females; viewing males committing sodomy with females or males; viewing girls with penises; observing girls smelling their panties or wearing their panties on their head or face; observing sadomasochism activities, etc.

In most cases, male porn addicts are motivated to observe all of the above-cited behaviors because they are seeking to behold a person of sexual affection in a humiliated condition. Much of this desire to observe such humiliating experiences is fueled by past social or sexual rejection, sexual abuse, or unresolved anger related to social rejection. Or, some male porn addicts desire to view such taboo/ fetish behaviors because a sense of intimacy with the sexual object or person of sexual affection is conceived in the male viewer's mind that empowers him, and/or bridges himself with desired intimacy. For instance, observing an object or person of sexual affection in certain behaviors of vulnerability is the *motivating high* that is associated with experiencing intimacy as a fantasy. In reference to sadomasochism viewing, some male porn abusers are motivated to observe such behaviors in order to affirm male dominance, potency and social control over sexual objects or persons of sexual affection in social reality – are not realized or never will be conceived.

## Pedophilia (Lust for Purity)

Some male abusers of pornography are into viewing pornography that depicts naked male or female children and preteens. The likely motivational origin for this preference is the lustful desire for having access to sexual objects or persons of sexual affection that represent purity. For those male porn addicts that prefer this type of fantasy, they can view the naked child or preteen as available for sex without any relational and cultural resistance, along with experiencing a pure intimacy with the sexual object or person of sexual desire because a child or preteen holds far more innocence than any adult object of sexual desire. In addition, the child or preteen object of sexual desire might become a target of fantasy because the male porn addict has experienced a past intimate conversation or close physical proximity of space (without sexual contact - yet desiring such contact) with the identified person of sexual affection.

## Auto-Asphyxiation

Some male abusers of pornography enjoy cutting-off their oxygen supply while masturbating through the use of either: placing a plastic bag over their head, tightening a rope around their neck, placing apples or oranges in their mouth, or a smoking a large amount of cigarettes. The limited amount of oxygen during the masturbation process creates a greater sense of heightened orgasm when the orgasm is achieved. Unfortunately, auto-asphyxiation is extremely dangerous and some men have died from their sedulous implementation of this process during masturbation activity.

# Chapter 3
## The Active Sexual Fantasy Life: Why?

So much use and abuse of pornography by males is motivated by the need for an active sexual fantasy life. Similarly, there are various explanations for understanding why males need an active sexual fantasy life through pornography use and abuse, and in this chapter, I will offer some of those explanations.

## Youth Validation

For those males ages thirty and up, there is the very real fact of lost youthfulness and with this forfeiture of virility and aging - derives the loss of certain motivating sexual hormones (specifically testosterone) and other physical liabilities experienced that inhibit sexual libido and performance such as: an enlarged prostate gland; obesity; loss of muscle build; hernia; diabetes; ulcers; kidney failure; pulmonary problems; high blood pressure; lower back pain; narrowing arteries; colon cancer, etc. In addition, all of these cited physical changes and maladies have a huge impact upon a man's ability to gain and maintain an erection; or at times, even initiate and sustain a sexual desire and consistent sexual drive. Likewise, it's then only logical to comprehend why some males in this age group desire to live vicariously through pornography. In addition, viewing images of youthful females or males may help stimulate a moribund sex drive and/or a longer-lasting erection - thereby validating a male porn addict's identity as a viable sexual being. If and when males of this age group begin to lose their sexual drive and ability to perform, this becomes a time for a huge identity crisis as a sexual being, and often times, instills a massive blow to their self-esteem and sexual identity as well!

## The Desire for Multiple Partners

There are some male users and abusers of pornography who find themselves in dead-end relationships (casual, boyfriend/girlfriend or marriage) that are not psychologically or sexually fulfilling and they are consequently compelled to search for other sexually satisfying relational options - hence the use of pornography serves as a temporary outlet to realize the legitimate psychological desire to have access to satisfying or multiple sexual partners. Or, some males are simply not able to realize contentment with one sexual partner and possess an authentic desire and need to have access to multiple sexual partners in order to achieve numerous pleasurable experiences - even if such access is fantasy-driven rather than reality-based. For many males who desire multiple partners, they are afflicted with the problem of *lustful eyes*; in other words, they inordinately love female or male physical beauty and are addicted to such loveliness and can never get enough satisfaction from viewing it! It's an endless cycle of addiction that precludes sexual fulfillment through a relational commitment to one person. Again, habitually accessing pornography provides a means for fulfilling the need to have access to sexual pleasure through multiple beautiful partners and such lusting will lend itself to motivating some male porn addicts toward purchasing thousands of pornographic magazines, videos or access to Internet porn sites (over a lifetime) in their quest to quench their idolatry for physical beauty.

## The Need for Power Implementation

Some male users and abusers of pornography utilize pornography as a fantasy opportunity to fulfill the implementation of power in a sexual relationship. Ostensibly in this case scenario, the male pornography user or abuser more than likely has no real social or sexual power in a sexual relationship, and therefore, pornography viewing offers a fantasy outlet for the implementation of such power in a sexual relationship.

## Relational Access and Self-Acceptance

For some male users and abusers of pornography, observing pornography allows the opportunity for relational access and self-acceptance through an outlet of fantasy. In many instances, those males with limited access to real-life social and sexual experiences are at high-risk for pornography use and abuse.

## High Libido/Sexual Frustration

Some males' use and abuse pornography as a fantasy outlet for relieving a high sexual drive - a compelling drive that is not being relieved with real-life opportunities for sexual relationships. Particularly vulnerable for having a high sexual libido and experiencing sexual frustration are males' ages: 13-30 simply as a result of their powerful sex drive motivated by a healthy hormonal system and because of their limited life experiences in reference to knowing how to initiate and maintain sexual relationships.

## The Need to Humiliate: Nudity, Vulnerable Positions and Body Fluids

As cited earlier, one of the driving motivational forces for explaining male pornography use and abuse is the need to humiliate sources of beauty and sexual objects and persons of affection - that in reality - can never be realized. In fact, in this type of case scenario, pornography use and abuse is a coping mechanism for unresolved anger and social rejection. In many cases, sexual fantasies that seem to assist with anger reduction and coping with social rejection are those fantasies that humiliate the sexual object or person of sexual affection. Moreover, some males will go to extreme measures in order to experience the ultimate orgasmic highs associated with applying humiliation upon the sexual object or person of sexual affection such as: viewing males or females in the following vulnerable positions: females with spread opened vaginas; males ejaculating; females or males having their face or other body parts ejaculated upon; males and females being sodomized; males and females spreading open their anus; females and males in the act of urination or defecation; males and females drinking their own urine or eating their own feces; males and females drinking the urine of others or eating the feces of others, etc.

## False Intimacy: Vicarious Experiences without Real Attachment

Some males do not realize that their use and abuse of pornography is related to the need to experience a sense of intimacy with fantasized sexual objects or persons of sexual affection in lieu of a real sexual experience or relationship that cannot be realized (Schaumburg 1997). Initially, in this case scenario, male pornography use begins in order to serve the fantasy purpose of achieving a sense of intimacy. Then, over a period of time, this behavioral practice evolves into an addictive state where men no longer are utilizing the pornography to achieve the fantasy of intimacy, but rather, are resigned to the fact that a sexual experience or relationship with an object or person of sexual affection will never become a reality. Likewise, the pornography addiction ultimately morphs into a vehicle for expressing anger through the humiliation of the preferred and unattainable sexual object or person of sexual affection as identified in the male's mind.

## No Real Desire for Intimacy

Some males use or abuse pornography simply because they have no real desire for sexual intimacy in a relationship because having such a relationship often requires other areas of commitment that they're not willing to experience. Therefore, viewing pornography offers these types of males' access to experiencing sexual orgasm without any relational costs and commitments.

## Taboo High: Body Fluids, Pedophilia, Incest, Sodomy, Panties and Animal Sex

Some males pornographic fantasies associated with achieving sexual orgasm are primarily associated with the *taboo-high:* the greater the pornographic image or video depicting taboo sexual behavior - the more intense the orgasmic high! It's more than likely that most taboo-highs required for achieving sexual orgasm have evolved from a previous lower level of pornography use and abuse of certain images; images that were deemed by the male user or abuser as no longer effective in stimulating exciting sexual orgasmic experiences. Therefore, some males are involved with taboo activities that assist with elevating the level of sexual orgasm achieved through pornography use and abuse by viewing the following taboo pornographic images or scenes: males and females urinating or defecating; males and females urinating and defecating on other persons; males and females eating feces or drinking urine; nude children and preteens in various natural or lewd poses; incest scenes: mothers and daughters, fathers and daughters, mothers and sons or fathers and sons having sexual relations with each other or participating in an orgy; sisters having sexual relations with each other or participating in orgy; other family members involved in incestuous activities; females and males being sodomized; little girls, preteens or women playing with their anus or smelling their own panties, males or females having sex with animals, etc.

In summation, male pornography addiction is very hard to eradicate once the addiction becomes full-blown in physiological desire and psychological meaning – particularly in reference to those males that are driven by fantasy urges that cannot be realized in reality - for whatever the reason. In addition, some male users of pornography will continue to purchase larger volumes of pornography because past viewed images lose their novelty; and novel pornographic images excite and aid certain male users toward realizing the optimum sexual orgasm they're desiring.

# Chapter 4
## Pornography Addiction and Those Consequences Associated with Areas of Being Human

There are many life consequences for those males that habitually abuse pornography.

I will briefly examine some of the major life consequences associated with such behavioral activity in light of the five areas of being human. Again, there are far more life consequences than those I have delineated in this section; however, those following consequences delineated are the more severe ones.

## Spiritual

According to the Old Testament book of Proverbs, people's lives are cut short when they pursue habitual wickedness. Proverbs 15:10 states: "Correction is grievous unto him that forsaketh thy way: and he that hateth reproof shall die." Also, Proverbs 10:27 says: "The fear of the Lord prolong days: but the years of the wicked shall be shortened."

According to Proverbs 19:3, behavioral folly ruins life – a foolish man rages against the Lord and blames him for his own self-destruction. Proverbs 19:3 states: "A man's own folly ruins his life, yet his heart rages against the Lord."

In addition, a loss of self-control always bring mass calamity upon a man's personal life. According to Proverbs 25:28: "Like a city whose walls are broken down, is a man who lacks self-control."

Also, excessive pornography abuse by the male person makes his heart and eyes impure – thereby polluting all of his heart-intentions with defilement and a debasement toward fellow human beings.

Certainly, there are other Old Testament scriptures that outline the Almighty Lord God's displeasure and wrath toward sexual perversion and sinful behaviors such as those found in Leviticus 18:6-23 and Deuteronomy 5:18-21, 27:20-22.

Lastly, when a man lives in sin, he forsakes his relationship with the Almighty Father God. There are numerous Old Testament and New Testament scriptures that attest to that very fact.

## Physical

There are a number of physiological consequences associated with pornography addiction that males should be mindful of. First, excessive masturbation might contribute to a lessening of sexual desire or erectile dysfunction. Second, excessive masturbation may also contribute to penile exhaustion (the inability to gain and sustain an erection) and nerve damage to the head of the penis. Moreover, inordinate masturbation may contribute to chronic bladder infections, prostate infections or prostrate enlargement, lower back pain or even cause a hernia. Lastly, if a male masturbator is practicing auto-asphyxiation (as a result of smoking cigarettes or using other procedures to cut-off his oxygen supply during masturbation), he runs the risk of collapsing a lung, contracting bronchitis, emphysema or lung cancer, or experiencing a cerebral hemorrhage or ruptured aortic aneurysm.

## Sociological

According to the Book of Proverbs 17:12, meeting a man in the midst of his folly (pornography use or abuse) can create potential interpersonal conflict or far greater short or long-term consequences for either person involved in a social structural relationship. Proverbs 17:12 says: "Let a bear robbed of her whelps meet a man rather than a fool in his folly."

From an economic perspective, the Book of Proverbs 17:20 indicates that a perverse heart does not prosper. Proverbs 17:20 states: "He that hath a froward heart findeth no good..."

Moreover, according to the Book of Proverbs 21:17, loving pleasure will make you poor. Prov. 21:17 states: "He who loves pleasure will become poor, whoever loves wine and oil will never be rich." In the case of the male pornography addict, his pleasure is pornography, and he spends thousands of dollars throughout the years of his addiction feeding his uncontrolled need for orgasmic pleasure.

Also, pornography abusers will bring forth trouble upon their families by sowing relational strife, undermining husband and wife sexual relations in the bedroom, and depleting economic resources. According to Proverbs 11:29: "He who brings trouble on his family will inherit only the wind, and the fool will be servant to the wise." Also, according to Proverbs 14:1: "The wise woman builds her house, but with her own hands the foolish one tears her down." In this case, the foolish one tearing the wise woman down is the wayward husband addicted to pornography who cannot even find the passion to make love to his wife or stop wasting economic resources on access to porn.

## Psychological Consequences

### Guilt

The male pornography abuser has to lead a double-life in order to conceal his behavioral activities - which if found out - may be viewed as extraordinarily unacceptable by family, friends, employers, co-workers, the general public, etc. Therefore, the male pornography addict more than likely will feel a consistent sense of guilt associated with the fact that's his public and private selves are divided by hypocrisy and his private life is laden with hidden immoral behavior.

## Fear

The male pornography user or abuser maybe consumed with the fear of being discovered by family, friends, co-workers, employers, etc. Likewise, the male pornography addict has to take great care in making sure that his stash of porn materials or use of porn Internet sites are not discovered – thereby disgracing himself and his family and losing community respect. Moreover, if the male porn addict is a semi-moral or moral person who does attend religious services of any kind, then he must also live with the constant fear of what the Almighty Lord God's anger retribution will be in response to his disobedient ways.

## Anger

By continuing to utilize pornography as an outlet for projecting anger toward sexual objects and/or persons of affection, the male pornography addict never resolves his anger issues and remains fixated in a dysfunctional habitual way of life that does nothing to help him move beyond his self-destructive fixation. Moreover, his interpersonal relationships and the general community will continue to suffer loss because he is less than the man he should be.

## Perception

In some cases, male abusers of pornography have a warped sense of reality regarding how they view other people as sexual beings. For instance, aided by the pornographic materials they view, some males may mistakenly believe that little girls, boys, preteens, teens, neighbors and coworkers etc. are always looking to find a suitable partner to have sex with in order to maximize their own pleasures in life. Similarly, with such a contorted sense of reality, some male porn addicts could potentially make an ignorant sexual advance toward an unwelcoming person and face pending criminal charges or social ostracism for such foolish behavior - all because their perceptual abilities have become jaded beyond the social rules of reality as a result of chronic pornography abuse.

## Vocational Consequences

Some male abusers of pornography are unable to focus upon the development of their own vocational actualization because their psychological obsession with pornography deadens their ability to perceive their own talents, abilities and opportunities. In addition, their pornography addiction itself precludes the dedicated time requisite for pursuing and realizing all of the behavioral activities associated with realizing vocational excellence.

# Chapter 5
## Biographic Interviews and Analysis

In this section, I will present some case scenarios associated with various comments made by American male users and abusers of pornography (ages:19-60) as cited by them via Internet chat commentary or in general interview conversations with them over the past twenty years. The names cited below are fictitious in order to protect identities but the races and professions indicated in each case scenario are authentic. All commentary cited either reflects feelings about pornography use or abuse, and/or plausible explanations for why pornography use/abuse occurs in association with viewing "only females" depicted. Most of the commentary outlined here has not been edited for the use of slang or graphic terms utilized in order to describe some deviant sexual experiences and physical body parts.

**Jim: White Male, 45-years-old, Real Estate Agent.**

"I can't believe that it's been thirty-three-years since I started looking at pornography.

I must have spent over $25,000 dollars on pornographic magazines since I have been eighteen-years-old. Since then, I have probably looked at over one hundred thousand photos of nude women in every possible pose imaginable. Over the last twenty years, it has been worse - simply because the woman depicted are far more beautiful and sexier than ever before! Plus, today, everything you see in porno now is so much more explicit - making my fantasies and orgasms that much greater! I mean come on, I'll never have any beautiful woman looking that sexy and gorgeous lying next to me – so what's a guy to do? I wish I could stop, and countless times I've said I will, but I have never been able to make that happen. I'm sure if you stacked up all of the pornographic magazines I have ever bought – the stack would be four or five building storeys tall or maybe even higher!"

## Mike: Black Male, 26-years-old, Student.

"For me using porn has always been about the sexual passion and never having an outlet. I mean what's a dude to do? For my generation, it's impossible to find a girl to date – either because at my age – every chick my age is married or too great to talk to! So what do I do to relieve my sexual passion? I'll either watch a porn DVD, go to Internet sites or buy a skin mag. If nothing is around for me to stimulate myself visually, I'll look around the house and find some other magazines, catalogs or newsprint sales-ads with beautiful women and get-off on those pics so as to get a good jerk-on. What other choice do I have? My sexual passion is too much to live without!"

## William: White Male, 51-years-old, College Professor.

"I have been looking at pornography since I was eight-years-old. For years, my whole lifestyle has been worrying about who will find my stash of porn. I remember when I was sixteen-years-old, I brought home some porn-mag pictures from work and stashed them underneath the hamper in the bathroom. However, for some reason, I forget about the stash and my mother found it. Later on, I learned to take better care of my stash because if my mother bagged me again - I'd be screwed! Looking back since then, I'm still looking at porn and I have to keep hiding my stash from my live-in girlfriends. Somehow, I think all of the girlfriends I had in the past knew about my stash – yet nothing was ever said about it. Honestly, I just can't help it; I need to look at naked women besides just my girlfriend. She just isn't enough!"

## Samuel: White Male, (Unwilling to Reveal Age or Profession).

"I really don't understand – maybe I'm mental or something, but I've had sexual feelings toward females ever since I was in first grade. Maybe my Mom sexually molested me or something and I just can't remember it! I recall being in first grade and fantasizing about how hot my classmate Lisa Mason was and how much I wanted to see her naked vagina! Then, when I was in third grade, I was hot for my teacher Ms. Ochenco! She was around twenty-five-years-old and she would always wear these pretty skirts and nice tops that showed cleavage. I remember she had this one blue top that she wore with little anchors on the lapels and that top would partially show cleavage associated with her pretty little teets! Man, was I dying to get in the sack with her! That's just the way I thought and I was 8 years old! All throughout elementary school, I would fantasize about seeing the girls I thought attractive in the nude. Obviously that way of thinking is still with me today – far beyond my elementary school days. For instance, even now, when I see a pretty female – whether a high school girl, college professor, coworker, or some girl at the mall, I'm still sweating to see that hot female chick naked! I'm thinking that's why porn is such a fantasy outlet for me. I know in reality I can't see my fantasy girls in the nude, but I can project that desire into the visuals I'm seeing in a DVD or on the Internet and get some relief for this insatiable fix!"

## Steven: White Male, 54-years-old, Sales Manager.

"I think some of my porn addiction is connected with anger issues toward the opposite sex as a result of a troubling photo I saw years ago in a magazine while at the barbershop as a little kid. I might have been around eight or nine-years-old at the time. The picture was of a beautiful girl clad in a bikini running on a beach with four naked little boys who each were maybe around five-years-old. Man, was I really pissed-off about that! I thought to myself, "why isn't that chick in the nude herself?" I really hated that chick in the bikini because she was humiliating the boys! I thought she deserves to be humiliated too, but there wasn't anything I could do about it! I was powerless to degrade that chick and helpless to do anything about the humiliation I felt for my male comrades! Likewise, I have been using porn for years to get-off and I really take pleasure in looking at naked women and observing them in all kinds of hilariously exposed positions while making fools of themselves! It kind of gives me some vindication from that profound sense of humiliation I felt for myself and male comrades years ago - when I saw that picture in the barber shop. The thing is: nothing seems to take away the scar of that humiliation I felt years ago. If anything, my need to view more and more pornography seems incapable of extinguishing my need to continue to humiliate beautiful women."

## Jose: Hispanic Male, 19-years-old, Student.

"My fascination with the female body started when I was young maybe around eight. My sister who was around twelve was very beautiful and we would watch TV together. She would sit on the couch with her legs up and her panty crotch showing. Man, did she look smoking hot! I could see her pubic hairs around her panty crotch and I would just fantasize about how gorgeous that body looked! Sure I was ashamed, but how could I deny the passion that I had as a result of observing something so gorgeous and sexy. Later on throughout the years, I saw my sister nude a couple of times by accident and would always fantasize about wanting to make love to her - not only because she was hot - but because we were actually close friends! I think some of my obsession for porn has been fueled by my unmet sexual lust I had for my sister's body when I was young, along with the fact that at that time - I wanted to make love to her and be sexually intimate with her - yet couldn't because of the incest taboo thing!"

## Mylo: Black Male, 41-years-old, Electrician.

"I have been looking at pornography for thirty years – too long actually. It's a habit I would love to break but I really don't have much else for gaining sexual pleasure. My wife doesn't like showing her body – I guess she's ashamed of it – and my sex life has always sucked! I don't think I've ever had a sexual orgasm induced by another partner. So, pornography helps me achieve orgasm and the more explicit and taboo the images - the better in helping me achieve orgasm!"

## Kevin: White Male, 37-years-old, (Unwilling to Reveal Profession).

"I like pornography images, videos or Internet sites that show females in a public nudity scenarios or in some kind of nude pageant or nudist camp. I think I have a penchant for this type of pornography because it demystifies and renders female beauty impotent under the reality of exposure and humiliation."

**Kurt: Black Male, 45-years-old, Autoworker.**

"Female beauty has always intrigued me. Actually I have been somewhat intimidated by it ever since high school. I enjoy watching DVD's of a woman taking shooting semen (from a man) in the face or looking at pictures of a woman's face covered in semen.

I think I take pleasure in viewing these kind of images or sexual activity because I think some women are way too gorgeous and hold way too much power because of their beauty. Therefore, what's a better way to get some relief from such a social injustice than to gunk these girls face with some white cream? After seeing their images covered in gunk, I feel some relief and a little revenge. Sometimes, rather than viewing images of creamed female faces, I'll cream on the faces of females in a porn magazine or on female faces in beauty magazines. I don't care as long as that beauty gets humbled with some tribute cream!"

**Sidney: White Male, 39-years-old, Engineer.**

"For some reason I'm attracted to girls that are ages eight to thirteen years old. To me nothing is more rocking hot than looking at these young girls beautiful faces, tender budding breasts and lovely developing hips and buttocks – along with the fact of their sexual innocence – what a compelling temptation! I have been viewing pornography for years in order to help relieve my sexual fantasies about preteen girls. What I'll do is find pictures of preteen girls in magazines and paste their faces over the female models faces in porn magazines so I can get an idea of what these young chicks might look like in the buff. I know it sounds sick, but I really don't understand why I find these girls far sexier and attractive than women my age? Luckily for me, I never married and had daughters because I don't think I could have controlled myself."

**Winslow: Black Male, 22-years-old, Customer Service Rep.**

"I look at pornography, but the bigger turn on for me is sniffing a teen girl or a woman's used panty crotches. I think the high for me is looking at pretty chicks and wondering what their privates smell like? It's always on my mind when I'm looking at or talking to a beautiful young girl or woman. I'm not sure whether my fetish preference is motivated by anger or by curiosity. I think it is more the result of curiosity because I know that after I find a girl's panties to smell that I dig, I don't want to perform that same behavior again. The thrill is gone and the mystery is solved!"

**Phillip: White Male, 46-years-old,
(Unwilling to Reveal Employment).**

"I have been looking at porn for years and really the last twenty years, I have seen my need grow for greater explicit images and sexual activities. As crazy as this sounds, I now have a huge desire to view images or videos of women urinating or defecating. At first, it started out as just a curiosity, but as time went on, the meaning behind viewing such activities changed. For me now, that's the ultimate high - watching some Internet peep video of some beautiful girl in a restroom or bathroom taking a piss or dump. Great stuff! For me, it's great to see pretty chicks in such an exposed and vulnerable position. Look, there are hot chicks I work with that any dude would love to see in those private moments; I think it's the great equalizer because some of these broads don't give any of us dudes the time of day!"

**Stanley: Black Male, 28 years-old, Health Care Worker.**

"I don't why, but I'm really attracted to older women. I like buying pornographic materials or going to Internet sites that show older women in their forties or fifties naked. It is awesome watching these women spread their lovely holes and they're so sexy! When I see a sexy older woman at work or even on the street, I fantasize what her p/a must look like. I'm obsessed! I have even went as far as stealing my girlfriend's mother's panties out of the laundry because I was so attracted to her! I had to get close to her scent and it was such a turn-on for me to know that I was so close to her p/a and she never even knew!"

## Keith: Black Male 35-years-old, Warehouse Worker.

"I think my pornography usage is associated with being inundated by beautiful girls and women since I was a kid. I watched a lot of TV as a kid and would always want to screw all the lovely girls depicted on TV. Then later, my fantasies started going beyond TV to girls in my neighborhood, girls at school, and girls at work. And now, it's even my friends' daughters! Man, it's really sad but if my coworkers and friends really knew what kind of pervert I was, I wouldn't have any friends! I sometimes make two or three trips a week to buy porn DVD's and magazines at the Adult store near my apartment. Also, I'm spending a hundred bucks a month on four Internet porn sites. In fact, most times, I have to go to three different stores to buy porn because I don't want the clerks who work there thinking that I'm the *perv* I really am! Crazy huh! Nevertheless, it's useless try to hide my perviness because when I go to certain porn shops to get my supply, they already know me as a *regular* anyways! What a disgrace I am! I'm going broke and I can't stop!

I pray to God to bring this to a halt, but it just seems to get worse. I don't want to go to some Porn AA meeting or something. Who the hell could do that?"

## Robert: White Male, 60-years-old, Bank Executive.

"I have been viewing pornography for over forty-years and I would definitely have to say that I'm addicted. It killed my marriage and my kids think I'm sick. I never can get enough! And now, everything in porn is so explicit you just get addicted! I mean, you can see anything you want to get your rocks-off! Biggest thing for me though is realizing that I'm living a double-life. People at work think I'm so conservative because of my religious beliefs, but little do they know I'm a porno freak! I'm pretty much into everything: young girls, fetish videos, female masturbation scenes, lesbianism, jerking-off on pictures of sexy females in power, etc. Sometimes instead of pornography, I'll buy a Newsweek, Time or People magazine just to masturbate off on the face of female politicians, Hollywood or TV stars. Actually, I feel so much better after I do it! There's actually porn videos of guy's behaving in such a fashion in reference to creaming on female images in popular magazines. I wish I could stop, but I'm spending a couple hundred bucks a month on porn! Last week, I went to so many porno sites on the Internet - I killed my computer – it totally locked-up from viruses and spyware! Glad I'm not married –or I'd be bagged! Now my problem is: where will I be able to go to get my computer cleaned-up? Whoever cleans the computer is going to see all the sick sites I have been looking at. LOL, God must be punishing me!"

**Tomas: White Male, 28-years-old, Student.**

"I'm into chicks from other races. I like looking at porn that shows Asian, Black or Eastern Indian girls in all kinds of explicit poses. I grew up in an all-white neighborhood so when I went to college, my sexual interest opened-up to females of other races. I can't seem to ever get enough of looking at some gorgeous girl from an opposite race and wondering what it would be like to be with her sexually? I think porn relieves the sexual tension for me and gives me an opportunity to have access to so much beauty and diversity in fantasy that I never could realize in reality because of my race and shyness."

**Julio-Paul: Hispanic Male, 34-years-old,
Part-time Gas Service Attendant.**

"My pornography usage is definitely linked with boredom. Many times there's just nothing of interest to do but rub one out. Sometimes I might jack three times a day!

It's definitely pathetic and I keep telling myself - I need to find a girl, get married and settle down - but how can I do that when I can't even work full-time? Moreover, I get so much satisfaction from looking at porn! Plus, with the porn, I don't have to deal with the hassles of a relationship. I can have the sex, nudity and nastiness without the relational bullshit that goes with it! Also, a lot of married guys say that once you're married: "It's like going celibate!"They say, after the honeymoon is over, the wife's body isn't exciting to them anymore and they need something else. Most married guys don't want the mess of an affair so porn is their answer! I think if I was working steady, I might not be abusing porn so much."

### Ken: White Male, 48-years-old, Teacher.

"I started looking at porn to aid in my masturbation activities when I was thirteen-years-old. Gradually, I needed to find an additional help to increase the orgasmic high so as to make the masturbation more intense. Therefore, I started smoking cigarettes while looking at pornography in order to induce the auto-asphyxiation experience along with using marijuana to aid in heightening my perceptive capacities regarding what I was viewing. I've been practicing auto-asphyxiation for the past thirty-five years. I know I need to stop – my lungs are probably shot (even though I don't fully inhale) but I'm feeling the symptoms now as I close-in on fifty. I can't imagine looking at porn without a cigarette in my mouth. In my opinion, male porn usage is normal simply because God created the male to be the pursuer of the female in order to keep the human population in motion. In other words, males are *animals in clothes* despite that fact that we are living in the twenty-first century. Moreover, what are men to do? The global media frenzy and obsession with a bombardment of photos of beautiful women makes it impossible for most men to ignore; moreover, it only further induces guys' temptation to see females exposed and in vulnerable states. Yes, I know what I'm doing is not right, but I'm like millions of men across this globe – I'm doing what I have to do in order to relieve sexual passion and find a way to cope with being bombarded by gorgeous women in the workplace and through various media sources. Has it hurt my marriage? I would say yes, but porn's not the only thing that's hurt my marriage."

### Lance: Black Male, 24-years-old, Student.

"I would say most of my pornography use is when I'm under high stress or when I'm really depressed and feeling hopeless. It's a psychological outlet and physiological release for me. Being at college all-day-long and seeing all of these hot chicks running around, along with the fact that I feel like a failure (and can't get the time of day from any of these girls), motivates me to look at porn. It's a release – simple as that; and to tell you the truth – I don't feel guilty about it! It's a pornographic world! Look, at the glorification of women that men have to put up with on a day-to-day basis! It's asinine; and if you're a young dude, it especially plays on your sexual passion and puts you in a position where you have to get some relief! For that matter, thank God there is porn because I'd probably be raping some hot chick! If you talk to older dudes too, they would probably tell you they're sick of being tempted by all of these hot women. I don't know how some young or middle-aged guy could stay married or not want to be with another hot chick when he's surrounded by female beauty everywhere he goes: at school; at work; in his neighborhood; at the store; reading the newspaper ads; watching the tube, etc. No doubt porn serves a sane purpose –although I'm sure any guy can get easily addicted to it! I'm not at the addiction point yet, but if I don't find a job and get some self-esteem relief soon in my life, I could end-up alone and addicted to porn. I hope that don't happen to me like it has happened to other guys!"

**Stephen: White Male, 26-years-old, Unemployed.**

"I like watching porno DVD's of chicks having sex with chicks. I really don't know what's behind that preference. It just seems like something that I've always fantasized about. I used to work at a health club and would always fantasize about watching the hot girls showering with each other. Porn brings that fantasy to life for me!"

**Fernando: Hispanic Male, 52-years-old, Railroad Employee.**

"I have been looking at pornography for over forty-years and my preference is watching men dominate and control a sexual experience. I'm into sexual intercourse and anal intercourse scenes. Nothing is more sexually alluring for me than watching a girl take a big stick and moan in ecstasy! Porn isn't my whole life and doesn't control me, but I like to fantasize about other girls. Marriage gets old as far as the sex life goes – and most guys really want to have a relationship where they're in sexual control and the wife is willing to do other sexual thing besides lay there like she's dead!"

The previous biographies shared by some male users and abusers of pornography (pornographic material related to viewing females) serves to help the reader understand that some of the behavioral origins for porn use and abuse are primarily related to historical experiences (and/or perception of those experiences), the need for realizing a sense of intimacy, and emotions such as jealousy, anger and fear – which all are related to the need to humiliate the female object of sexual desire.

Some specific historical examples cited were related to long histories of using/abusing pornography in order to procure a sense of social or psychological relief due to social rejection or sexual frustration and/ or experiencing a history of sexual failure in initiating or sustaining fulfilling sexual relationships with women. Also, in reference to these sample subjects, personal and social structural biographical history played a significant role in determining an influential longstanding definition of beauty that holds a profound psychological power upon the male respondent's life. In addition, from a social structural point of analysis, male porn use/abuse reportedly serves as a fantasy outlet for unfulfilled sexual relationships of longing – whether desired at very young ages or in later teen or adult years. Porn use/abuse also was reported to be associated with compensating for unfulfilling sexual relationships or unrealized desires for experiencing sexual subjugating power over identified objects of sexual affection or persons of sexual affection. Lastly, a number of male respondents made reference to historical and cultural definitions of female beauty that could not be socially and psychologically reconciled with. It was also cited that early sexually longings with pure motives were blocked, due to cultural rules that define early sexual desire and behavior as taboo.

Again, there are certainly many other explanations for male pornography use and abuse than those biographically shared or analyzed here; however, the significant point of analysis that may be derived from these biographical accounts is that a thorough assessment utilizing the five areas of being human must be conducted before any precise knowledge might be applied to understanding the origins of male pornography use and abuse. Without such a thorough assessment, there can be little understanding of those viable therapeutic methods of treatment that might be applied to promote cessation and healing regarding serious male pornography addictions.

# Chapter 6
## The Process of Healing from Male Pornography Addiction

All five areas of being human must be applied as accurate tools of assessment in order to direct therapeutic treatment for understanding and treating the origins of male pornography addiction. However for brevity's sake, in this chapter, I will focus upon the spiritual area of assessment and treatment. Here I will apply the word of God from the Old and New Testament Bible to underscore the assessment and treatment process for laying a foundation for healing.

In reference to healing male pornography addiction, the male porn addict must first decide that he desires to receive healing from the addiction and be forever done with it! Without such a heart-commitment bent upon repentance, the male porn addict cannot even begin to receive the delivering power of Almighty God's word in order to realize change and healing. Therefore, in order to experience a desired heart that is on fire to apprehend change and healing, the male porn addict has to become educated toward understanding why using and/or being addicted to pornography is an offense to God, along with comprehending that it's self and community destructive! After that process of education has been understood, the male porn addict is then ready to read through those Old and New Testament Scriptures that offer the Holy Spirit's power of healing.

In truth, the process of spiritual healing begins with not isolating self further from social interaction but counting the cost of the addiction; focusing upon educating oneself in reference to the cost of self and community destruction, and resolutely deciding upon healing the inner man through the help of the Holy Spirit of God.

## Why Quit? The Old and New Testament Scriptures Underscore Why!

The supporting foundation for why any person should extricate him or herself from any addicting reality is because most addictions have costs imposed upon the human body. Moreover, according to the Biblical creation story as cited in the Book of Genesis Chapters 1-2, a human being has no willful decision in his creation. Therefore, any man living upon this earth must submit to the fact that his physical body is not his own. Likewise, we should take inventory of our faults and wicked ways (Psalm 10:13). According to Psalm 4:2, the human body is created in the image of God. Therefore, we should repent of our sins and fear Almighty God as instructed by Solomon in the Book of Ecclesiastes (Ecclesiastes 8:12-13).

Also, a man's perception of the world around him is either a light to his soul or a source of confusion and darkness. According to the teaching of Jesus Christ as cited in Luke 11:34: "The light of the body is the eye: therefore when thine eye is single, thy whole body also is full of light; but when thine eye is evil, thy body is full of darkness." Christ also taught as cited in Matthew 5:29: "And if thy right eye offend thee, pluck it out, and cast it from thee: for is it profitable for thee that one of thy members should perish, and not that thy whole body should be cast into hell." Ostensibly, Jesus is making reference to the seriousness of how our eyes perceive the world and such perceptions influence our spiritual heart condition. In addition, he makes reference to the fact that there is a place called "hell" ultimately associated with a final consequence of leading a lifetime of unrepentant impure perceptions/thoughts that motivate sinful behaviors. In addition, some of the impure and vile thoughts that motivate pornography use and abuse are earmarked in the Book of Deuteronomy and Leviticus as desirous sources that are dishonorable and heinous:

| | |
|---|---|
| Leviticus 18:6 | - No one is to approach any close relative to have sexual relations. |
| Deuteronomy 27:23 | - Cursed is the man who sleeps with his mother-in-law. |
| Leviticus 18:7 | - Do not dishonor your father by having sexual relations with your mother. She is your mother; do not have sexual relations with her. |

| | |
|---|---|
| Deuteronomy 27:20 | - Cursed is the man who sleeps with his father's wife, for he dishonors his father's bed. |
| Leviticus 18:9 | - Do not have sexual relations with your sister, either your father's daughter or you mother's daughter, whether she was born in the same home or elsewhere. |
| Deuteronomy 27:22 | - Cursed is the man who sleeps with his sister, the daughter of his father or the daughter of his mother. |
| Leviticus 18:10 | - Do not have sexual relations with your son's daughter or your daughter's daughter; that would dishonor you. |
| Leviticus 18:12 | - Do not have sexual relations with your father's sister; she is your father's close relative. |
| Leviticus 18:15 | - Do not have sexual relations with your daughter-in-law. She is your son's wife; do not have relations with her. |
| Leviticus 18:16 | - Do not have sexual relations with your brother's wife; that would dishonor your brother. |
| Leviticus 18:17 | - Do not have sexual relations with both a woman and her daughter. Do not have sexual relations with either her son's daughter or her daughter's daughter; they are her close relatives. That is wickedness. |
| Leviticus 18:19 | - Do not approach a woman to have sexual relations during the uncleanness of her monthly period. |

Leviticus 18:20       - Do not have sexual relations with your neighbor's wife and defile yourself with her.

Leviticus 18:22       - Do not lie with a man as one lies with a woman; that is detestable.

Leviticus 18:23       - Do not have sexual relations with an animal and defile yourself with it. A woman must not present herself to an animal to have sexual relations with it; that is a perversion.

Deuteronomy 5:18, 21 - You shall not commit adultery… You shall not covet your neighbor's wife.

Also, the case of personal idolatry is a major reason why pornography addiction should cease. Any image perpetually worshipped by a man draws him away from God and is placed upon the throne of his heart's desire above and beyond his passion for fellowship with his creator. Deuteronomy 5:8 states: "You shall not make for yourself an idol in the form of anything in heaven above or on the earth beneath or in waters below."

In truth, pornography worships women and men on earth. Yet, although many males love pornography, such an idolatrous love cannot save them. According to Judges 10:13-14: "But you have forsaken me and served other gods, so I will no longer save you. Go and cry out to the gods you have chosen. Let them save you when you are in trouble."

Also, the lust and love for women has the ability to turn a man away from God as chronicled in the life of King Solomon. 1 Kings 11:1-4 says: "King Solomon, however, loved many foreign women besides Pharaoh's daughter – Moabites, Ammonites, Edomites, Sidonians and Hittites. They were from nations about which the Lord had told Israelites, "You must not intermarry with them, because they will surely turn your hearts after their gods." Nevertheless, Solomon held fast to them in love. He had seven hundred wives of royal birth and three hundred concubines, and his wives led him astray. As Solomon grew old, his wives turned his heart after other gods, and his heart was not fully devoted to the Lord his God, as the heart of David his father had been."

Psalm 31:10 and Psalm 38:3-6 indicate that our guilt associated with our impurity and unholy state creates poor health. Also, Psalm 39:9 and Deuteronomy 28:15-29 instruct us that there is judgment for our sins and idolatrous ways.

What's most important is that if we live in unrepentant behavioral ways, the wrath of God can flare-up anytime against us to impose just punishment or instruction during the course of our living lives. (Psalm 2:11-12).

## Spiritual Instruction for Overcoming the Male Pornography Addiction Madness: Psalms and Other Biblical Scriptures

According to Saint Paul, a major battle that humanity has with being imprisoned by evil is how we perceive and think about the world that interacts with us and surrounds us. Therefore, Paul instructs us to gain control over our thought life. In his letter to the Philippians (4:8), Paul states: "Finally brothers, whatever is true, whatever is noble, whatever is right, whatever is pure, whatever is lovely, whatever is admirable - if anything is excellent or praiseworthy - think about such things."

In truth, male pornography addiction is living life like a prisoner. The jailer is pornography and the male addict's prison is his pornography addiction. However, the Almighty Lord God sees our afflictions and anguish of soul (Psalm 31:7). The power and compassion of the Almighty Lord God indicates that he is able to set prisoners free (Psalm 146:7, Psalm 25:15) for the Lord is capable of doing all things (Job 42:2). The male porn addict must cry for mercy to become free from the bondage of pornography (Psalm 6:9) and the Almighty Lord God will hear his cry and deliver him from this bondage (Psalm 3:8;

Psalm 18:1-6). Also the male porn addict must ask for forgiveness and it will be received by the Lord (Psalm 25:11, Psalm 65:3).

The male pornography addict should never forget that even when he falls as he wages his battle to overcome this heinous addiction, the Almighty Lord God is a refuge for the oppressed (Psalm 9:9) and does hear the prayers of the afflicted (Psalm 10:17, Psalm 22:24, Psalm 28:2). Moreover, the Almighty Lord God is able to assist the male porn addict with his willful sins and provide the power to help him repent (Psalm 19:13) and turn his historic spiritual darkness of addiction and bondage into light (Psalm 18:28).

King Solomon instructs us that there is "a time to heal" (Ecclesiastes 3:3), but in the case of the male pornography addict, that reality of *lasting healing* is related to allowing the Almighty Lord God to cleanse the heart from the desire of "want." Psalm 23:1 instructs us that: "I shall not want." One of the most powerful of temptations that motivates male pornography abuse is *wanting*. However, the Lord offers help and healing (Psalm 30:2). Likewise, the male porn addict needs the power of the Almighty Lord God to help him scale the wall (Psalm 18:2) of temptation that seeks to limit his vitality and potentiality as a viable and productive human being. Equally, fervent prayer can assist in helping the male pornography addict ask the Almighty Lord God to deliver unto him the desires of his heart (Psalm 20:4-5) that are pure and in congruence with the holy will of God.

The Almighty Lord God is also faithful in helping us understand our hidden faults and forgive us for those faults (Psalm 19:12) – something that the male pornography abuser needs desperately to realize in order to win the battle against pornography addiction.

When the male pornography addict is moving on his willful journey toward redemption and holiness, the Almighty Lord God will provide him blessings for his purity (Psalm 24:4-5); turn his despondent condition into dancing (Psalm 30:10-12), and remember not the sins of his youth (Psalm 25:7). Moreover, the Almighty Lord God perpetually instructs sinners in his ways so we have a guide for the future (Psalm 25:8).

The lifelong journey of healing from pornography addiction will never be without periodically confronting spiritual, physical and psychological weakness. Therefore, the male pornography addict should always confess his sins to the Almighty Lord God and others (Psalm 32:2-5) in order to remain guilt free. He should also pray daily for: the Almighty Lord God to create a pure heart within him (Psalm 51:10, Psalm 51:1); the establishment of truth in his innermost parts (Psalm 51:6); a willing heart to sustain him (Psalm (51:12), and to not allow anger to motivate willful sin (Psalm 4:4).

Lastly, the struggling male porn addict who aspires for freedom from spiritual bondage should cast his care upon the Lord (Psalm 55:22) and put his hope in God (Psalm 42:11) because God's faithfulness reaches the skies (Psalm 57:10) and the Lord God will provide help against the enemy because man's help is useless (Psalm 60:11). In truth and hope, we should all remember there is access to healing for all of us that lovingly desires to change our wicked ways (Psalms 40:1-4) and then, Almighty Father God will indeed heal us (Psalm 41:3-4).

# Chapter 7
## Therapeutic Assessment Questions

The following questions relate to any of the five areas of being human – the primary tool of assessment for helping to understand the origins of any human behavior. Therefore, any therapist looking to understand the origins and extent of a male's pornography use or addiction would be prudent to ask the following questions:

## Spiritual Questions

Do you believe in God? If so, explain why? If not, explain why?

How often do you ponder the origins of life or the origins of events that surround you?

Do you believe that bad things happen to people that behave terrible things?

What kinds of behavior do you consider immoral?

Do you consider pornography use/abuse immoral? If not, why not?

What do you consider about pornography to be beneficial to your spiritual condition?

Do you believe pornography is beneficial to the community? If so, how?

If you believe in God, how do you believe he views your usage or abuse of pornography?

## Physiological Questions

Do you believe you're sexual attractive? If so, explain why? If not, explain why?

How often do you feel the need to masturbate?

How often do you actually masturbate on a daily or weekly basis?

How would you describe the intensity of your masturbation orgasms?

Do you have any form of erectile dysfunction?

How would you describe your overall health?

Do you have any major health problems that hinder your sexual relational performance?

## Sociological Questions

### Historical

What type of quality of a relationship did you have with you mother, father, brother(s) or sister(s) when you were young?

While living with your family, were you ever sexually abused by a family member?

If a family member sexually abused you, what emotions do you feel about that experience now?

Have you experienced sexually satisfying relationships in the past?

### Social Structural

Are you currently involved in a sexually satisfying relationship?

What sexual behavioral act is most satisfying for you and why?

Do you experience intimacy when you have sexual relations with another person? If so, why? If not, why not?

Do you view sexual relations as an opportunity for you to experience control or collaboration?

Is there a person that you desire to have sexual relations with that you formerly had sexual relations with before?

Is there a person who you desire to have sexual relations with but having such an experience would be considered unlawful such as: mother, father, son, daughter, sister, brother, child, another's spouse, an underage person and/or other extended family members?

If you desire to have sexual relations with a member of your immediate or extended family, when did this desire originate, and what do you believe might be the origins of such a desire?

Do you spend a lot of your energy keeping your pornography use/ abuse a secret?

Do you have any sexual fantasies regarding underage persons or family or extended family members?

Is your life filled with consistent encouragement or praise?

How well do you respond to encouragement or praise?

## Cultural

What do you do for recreation and leisure?

How do you believe society views pornography use/abuse?

Are you a pornography addict? If so, explain why? If not, why not?

What cultural beliefs or forms of mass media have impacted your use of pornography?

What type of physique do you prefer in a sexual partner?

What sexual behavioral acts do you consider deviant?

Do you believe that the civil laws that you currently live under are fair and just in determining who you can have sexual relations with? If not, why not?

## Economic

How much money do you spend on pornography on a monthly basis?

Do you ever spend money on pornography that was budgeted for some other living expense?

Do you believe you are overworked?

## Political

What are your stake issues for using/abusing pornography?

What are your stake issues for masturbating?

When do you feel most compelled to masturbate with pornography as a stimulating aid?

## Institutional

Do you have criminal record?

Have you ever been convicted of a sexual crime?

Have you ever committed a sexual crime but it was never found out or received a conviction?

## Environmental

Do you live in a family or solitary?

How would you describe the social interaction style of your current family relationships?

What is your neighborhood like: friendly, secure, criminal or anonymous?

Do you have any close male or female friendships?

Is there a person in your social environment who you would like to have sexual relations with, yet that person is unaware of your social presence and/or desire?

## Psychological Questions

Do you use pornography to express anger? If so, explain how?

Do you use pornography to feel in control? If so, explain how?

What role does pornography play in helping you to fulfill fantasies?

Do you feel guilty about using porn?

What fears do you have about your life?

Are there any sexual fantasies you have about women or men?

Describe your ideal sexual partner.

What are the origins of your sexual fantasies regarding women or men?

Do you hate girls or women? If so, why?

Do you hate boys or men? If so, why?

Do you love girls or women? If so, why?

Do you love boys or men? If so, why?

Do you hate girls, women, boys or men for being sexually attractive? If so, why?

Do you hate yourself? If so, why?

Do you feel emptiness in your life? If so, what is that emptiness related to?

## Vocational Questions

What are your vocational aspirations?

What is impeding you from achieving your vocational aspirations?

What are your life dreams?

Are you satisfied with your work role?

What are your natural abilities?

How often do you express or use your natural abilities?

What are your interpersonal strengths?

What are your interpersonal weaknesses?

What do you desire to learn that you do not know now?

What additional skills would you like to learn that you do not know now?

# Bibliography

Gideon's International Bible. 1998. Nashville, Tennessee.

Holy Bible: New International Version. 1978. Grand Rapids, Michigan: Zondervan Bible Publishers.

King James Bible. 1998. USA: Oxford University Press.

Schaumburg, Harry. 1997. *False Intimacy.* Colorado Springs, Colorado: NavPress Publishing Group.

Sharts, Thomas, D. 2007. *The American Deception.* Philadelphia, PA: Xlibris Inc.